REVOLUTION

AUTHOR: CHRISTOPHER MAYNARD   CONSULTANT: DR. TIM SHAKESBY

DEAR READER,

THEY WERE NOISY. THEY WERE MESSY. THEY WERE EVEN BLOOD-CURDLING. BUT *THE HISTORY NEWS* WAS ALWAYS THERE IN THE THICK OF THINGS — DOCUMENTING WHAT HAPPENED AS THE WORLD'S GREATEST REVOLUTIONS ERUPTED INTO LIFE.

BRAVING ALL KINDS OF DANGER, OUR REPORTERS STAYED WITH EVENTS AS, NATION BY NATION, PEOPLE CRIED "ENOUGH!" AND TOSSED OUT THEIR FORMER LEADERS. THESE ARE STORIES OF LIBERTY AND JUSTICE BUT ALSO OF VIOLENCE. THEY ARE STORIES OF DREAMS COME TRUE AND DREAMS TURNED TO DUST, FOR REVOLUTIONS OFTEN HAVE RESULTS THAT NO ONE EVER IMAGINED.

WHATEVER THEIR OUTCOME, EACH OF THESE REVOLUTIONS CAME ABOUT BECAUSE ORDINARY PEOPLE RAN OUT OF PATIENCE AND DEMANDED TO BE HEARD. *THE HISTORY NEWS* HAS PUT TOGETHER THIS VERY SPECIAL EDITION TO PAY TRIBUTE TO THEIR COURAGE.

THE EDITOR-IN-CHIEF

Christopher Maynard

A NOTE FROM OUR PUBLISHER

Of course, *The History News* didn't exist when these revolutions took place. But if it had, we're sure that it would have been the newspaper everybody was reading! We hope you enjoy reading it, too.

Candlewick Press

CANDLEWICK PRESS
CAMBRIDGE, MASSACHUSETTS

CONTENTS

WHAT IS A REVOLUTION?

IF YOU WAKE UP ONE MORNING TO FIND YOUR FELLOW COUNTRYMEN ARE MARCHING THROUGH THE STREETS, OR STORMING ROYAL PALACES, OR PROPPING PRESIDENTS UP IN FRONT OF FIRING SQUADS, CHANCES ARE, THEY ARE HAVING A REVOLUTION.

AT ITS SIMPLEST, A REVOLUTION IS A GREAT UPHEAVAL WHEN ONE KIND OF GOVERNMENT GETS FLUNG OUT AND A COMPLETELY NEW ONE TAKES ITS PLACE. MOST OFTEN IT GETS PRETTY VIOLENT, FOR OLD LEADERS CLING TO POWER LIKE BARNACLES. BUT NOT ALWAYS! THERE HAVE BEEN REVOLUTIONS — RARE ONES — THAT TOOK PLACE WITH LITTLE BLOODSHED. OTHERS, HOWEVER, COST THE LIVES OF MANY MILLIONS.

THE REVOLUTIONS WE HAVE CHOSEN FOR THIS SPECIAL EDITION OF *THE HISTORY NEWS* ARE THE CLASSIC ONES. NOT ONLY DID THEY INVENT A NEW SET OF RULES IN ONE COUNTRY, THEY ALSO CHANGED WHAT PEOPLE ALL OVER THE WORLD THOUGHT ABOUT THE WAY THEY WERE GOVERNED.

TEA OVERBOARD IN BOSTON HARBOR

Illustrated by CHRIS MOLAN

TEA TIME: In an act of defiance over British taxes, protesters disguised as Mohawk Indians destroy an entire cargo of tea by tossing it into Boston Harbor.

AMERICANS DIDN'T TURN to revolution overnight. It took years of British blundering to bring them to the boiling point. At the Boston Tea Party in 1773, our Massachusetts reporter discovered they were angry enough for action.

ON THE CLEAR, cold night of December 16, 1773, with a bright moon shining on the water, a crowd of Boston citizens boarded three tea ships moored in the harbor.

Many were disguised as Mohawk Indians. All were hopping mad. Whooping and hollering, they broke open 342 chests of tea and dumped the contents overboard. It was low tide, and salty, dark tea was soon staining the shore.

Hundreds of people gathered to watch this late night "tea party." Afterward, they set off with all the disguised protesters and marched in triumph through Boston.

To a man, the crowd has vowed to fight the hated tax on tea that Britain is trying to make people pay. The colonies now refuse to drink British tea — this tax, they claim, is extremely unfair.

NO TAXES WITHOUT OUR SAY

For some years now, Britain has levied tax after tax on the American colonies to make them pay a share of her huge debts — and to stamp her authority firmly on this side of the Atlantic. Yet few here care to be milked in this high-handed way. People are demanding a say in what taxes are collected and how they are spent.

In the meantime, the governor has vowed to bring Boston to heel. Ever since the tea ships arrived in November, he has refused to let them return to England until every last penny of tax on their cargo is paid. With both sides refusing to budge, there was bound to be a showdown.

This morning, furious officials at the governor's mansion promised to find out who the tea-pouring "Mohawks" were. But the several hundred Bostonians who know the protesters well show no sign of turning them in.

This can only mean that the King and his ministers will be madder than ever. Rumors are flying that they want to close the port to punish all Boston until the tax and the lost tea are paid for. They may even be preparing to send over troops to teach the Colonists a lesson they'll never forget!

NIGHT RIDE: Revere warns Lexington patriots that British troops are on the way.

REDCOATS ON THE RUN!

Illustrated by STEVE NOON

THE BOSTON TEA PARTY stirred things up. But the spark for war was a clash between the minutemen, a rag-tag citizens' army, and a troop of British redcoat soldiers outside Boston in April 1775. Our reporter talked to hero of the day, Paul Revere.

? Mr. Revere, how did you get involved?

I'm a silversmith by trade, but I'm also an American patriot. I help out by riding to deliver messages. We patriots say the British have no right to walk all over us. Ever since they stationed soldiers in Boston, they have been spoiling for a fight. Well, today we stood up to them!

? How did it all start?

We heard they wanted to attack our arms supplies at Concord, 21 miles or so from Boston. Last night, 700 soldiers set off on a raid. Will Dawes and I galloped ahead to warn our boys that the redcoats were coming.

We rode to Lexington first and got to the village at midnight. Doctor Sam Prescott, another patriot, joined us there. When a British patrol cut us off, Sam got past and raised the alarm in Concord.

? When were the first shots fired?

The redcoats got to Lexington first, fired on a small force of minutemen who tried to block the way, and killed eight. Then they marched on to Concord. By then we'd hidden our supplies.

The soldiers found nothing and started back to Boston. Meanwhile, our boys had spread out along the road and began to pepper them from the trees. A long line of scarlet is a hard target to miss! I heard we shot 250 of them!

? Does this mean war?

They fired first. Now we've shown the strongest army in the world we can give as good as we get. If they want war, so be it! ⓨ

MEET THE MAN WHO'S TAKING A STAND

DIVORCE: Delegates from all 13 colonies sign the Declaration of Independence (left). The colonies are now calling themselves states.

Peter Newark's American Pictures

ON JULY 4, 1776, delegates from the 13 colonies met to approve a Declaration of Independence. On August 2, they signed it. At last the long-awaited divorce has begun. Leading delegate Thomas Jefferson spoke to *The History News.*

YOU KNOW, we've been fighting the British for over a year now. Even so, we never stopped trying to settle things peacefully. But our every offer was ignored. The King refused to take us seriously.

It was decision time. That's why delegates from the colonies met here in Philadelphia, to vote for independence.

We hated the British meddling with our trade, driving us out of business with endless taxes and regulations. Worse, we had no voice in how we are ruled — unlike the men of Britain, who have Parliament to represent them. And then an army was sent over to crush us as if we were hooligans. Well, enough is enough!

RISKING ALL FOR LIBERTY

So the delegates drafted a short statement of our intentions. I had the honor of writing much of what we're calling our "Declaration of Independence." In it we say why we have broken with Britain. From now on, the former colonies will be states and will make their own way in the world.

But I'm proudest of the part where we state our beliefs. Listen.

"We hold these truths to be self-evident, that all men are created equal, that they are endowed by their Creator with certain unalienable Rights, that among these are Life, Liberty and the pursuit of Happiness."

Of course it's fine to make bold statements, but this is a matter of life or death. If the British beat us, all 56 of us who signed the Declaration will be tried for treason and hanged. But if all the colonies stick together, and if we find allies among other nations, we might hold our own in the coming war. I pray our soldiers are up to it! ▼

FOR OR AGAINST?

Our survey of public opinion in 1776 shows how little support there was for independence among the three million people who lived in America. Two out of three did not care for it.

☞ **30% were for independence (known as patriots)**

☞ **30% were against independence (known as loyalists)**

☞ **30% had no opinion or kept changing their mind depending how the fighting was going (known as fence-sitters)**

☞ **10% were too busy hunting and farming to reply. But after war broke out, support steadily increased.**

BIG CHILL: At Valley Forge, American troops suffered weeks of cold and disease. One in four died before the winter was out.

WINTER OF DISCONTENT

Illustrated by GINO D'ACHILLE

DECLARING independence was easy. Convincing the British to let go was a whole lot harder. In the bitter winter of 1777, the American army came within a whisker of losing the war.

THE BRITISH held the ports and were winning most of the big battles. But the American army, led by General George Washington, had an ace up its sleeve. It didn't have to win often. It just had to wear the British down—not an impossible challenge. Yet in the winter of 1777, Washington's soldiers nearly didn't make it.

TOO COLD TO FIGHT

As always, the fighting stopped as soon as the weather turned cold. The British made themselves nice and comfortable in the American capital, Philadelphia, which they had captured in the fall. Washington's army made camp at Valley Forge, some 19 miles northwest of the city.

For the first few weeks, the men huddled in tents as they built log cabins. Then the weather got worse and supplies ran low. Without pay or enough food, clothing, and blankets, the army suffered terribly. Not only that, many local farmers preferred to sell their produce to the British (who paid well for food).

Washington begged the politicians to send money and supplies. But the new states had little of either to spare.

Hunger and disease in the lice-infested cabins began to take their toll. Soldiers began to die by the hundreds.

Of the 12,000 men who set up camp, some 3,000 perished that winter. Many more deserted and went home. By spring, the soldiers could barely stand on their feet, let alone fight. Only Washington's strong will kept his troops with him to the end.

With the warmer weather came the good news for which everyone had been praying. France had at last declared war on her old rival, Britain, and was sending troops and ships to help the new states.

Valley Forge had been a close call. If George Washington hadn't held his army together, the Americans would have lost the war. ★

SEA WALL: French ships arrive and block British supplies.

Peter Newark's American Pictures

VICTORY AT LAST!

Illustrated by GINO D'ACHILLE

WASHINGTON stunned the world in October 1781 when he and his allies, the French, sprang a trap and captured 8,000 British soldiers at Yorktown. Our reporter sent us this eyewitness account.

FOR THREE heartbreaking years, the Americans have been struggling to beat the British. Last August, Washington heard his French allies were sending a fleet of warships to Virginia to blockade the British army camped there. It was his lucky break.

He quickly left the north, where he had been trying to push back the British, and headed south with an army of 18,000 American and French troops to meet the fleet. I rode with them.

WASHINGTON'S MOMENT OF GLORY

The men moved fast, determined to box in the British general, Lord Cornwallis, as he waited for fresh supplies at Yorktown.

By the end of September, the British were trapped. French ships cut off all escape by sea. Washington's troops began to tighten the noose on land.

On October 17, we learned Cornwallis had tried to ferry his men across a river the night before, in a desperate dash to safety. A storm blew back his boats, and he lost the will to fight.

Two days later, as a British band played "A World Turned Upside Down," Cornwallis's men trudged out of Yorktown and threw down their weapons.

Washington's troops laughed in amazement. Who'd have thought this homegrown army would one day accept the surrender of 8,000 crack British soldiers?

As I talked to American and French officers, they all praised the quick way General Washington had seen and grabbed his chance. "It was a masterpiece of military planning," claimed one major. "Only Washington could have pulled it off!" ◾

Ian Thompson

BEATEN: A quarter of the British army surrendered at Yorktown, Virginia. It was the last big battle of the war.

LOYALISTS BEAT A HASTY RETREAT

Illustrated by CHRIS MOLAN

HARD CHOICE: Fearing for their safety now that the war is over, about 100,000 loyalists are fleeing from their homes.

EARLY IN 1783, with Britain about to accept American independence, our reporter talked to a loyalist in Georgia who had stood by Britain all through the war.

❓ Why did you stay loyal to the King?
Britain helped us build a good life for ourselves here in America. In return for our loyalty, we were protected by the strongest nation in the world. We did just fine as colonies, and in my view, there was nothing to be gained by independence.

❓ Did you take part in the fighting?
No. I didn't want to fight with my neighbors and friends. When British troops came to Georgia in 1778, I was certain that we loyalists would rise up. We were so many, I expected us to set up a new government that would say "no" to independence and vote to stay British. I never expected such fierce fighting to break out between patriots and loyalists.

❓ Did you think Britain could win?
If French ships hadn't blocked supplies, it would have been easy for the British to hold the big towns. The towns could have become bases from which to beat General Washington's army.

❓ What did loyalists like you do after the British began to lose?
Bitter fighting broke out all around here between loyalists and patriots. Neighbors turned on each other, bent on murder and revenge. There was so much hatred on both sides that we could no longer live in peace together.

❓ Is that why you are leaving Georgia?
Yes. My business is in ruins and I fear for the safety of my family — far too many loyalist homes have been burned down. Almost every loyalist I know is planning to get out, and my family and I are sailing to Nova Scotia tomorrow to start a new life there. I'm brokenhearted. ▼

Bridgeman Art Library

GEORGE WASHINGTON: First a general, then a president.

THE RIGHT MAN FOR THE JOB!

PEACE RETURNED in 1783. But it was another six years before the country got the government it has today. In April 1789, *The History News* was in New York on the day George Washington became first president of the United States.

LAST MONTH, the elected leaders of the United States sat down to business. They had just one task—to find a president. The only name to fit the bill was George Washington, although a few doubted if a soldier would make a good leader in peace time. Could he heal the pains of war and could he govern the country firmly?

There's no doubt about his popularity. As Washington rode north to New York from his home in Virginia, people everywhere turned out to cheer him on. He was being sent to govern on a great wave of public support.

On the day of the swearing in, we all could see how nervous he was. He was never a great public speaker, and he shook with stage-fright as he read his speech!

Everybody we talked to agrees the president's biggest challenge is to weave 13 independent-minded states into a new nation. He is lucky to be helped in this by the way people are thinking of themselves as Americans. More and more they feel they are part of one great country. As my hackney cab driver said, "We're all Americans now, and always have been."

If all four million Americans share the president's vision of a United States that is strong, prosperous and free, this country will be a shining example to other nations for a great many years to come. ▼

AFTER THE REVOLUTION

THE AMERICAN REVOLUTION made the whole world sit up and take notice. Here's why.

FIRST, IT SHOWED how a young country with no army, navy or money could beat a mighty empire with fleets of ships, armies of soldiers and colonies all over the world.

Second, this new nation set up a new way of governing itself. Instead of kings and queens, it had a president and representatives, known as Congress, who were chosen by the people. It was the world's newest and biggest republic.

Above all, its voters were free and equal, and had the right to elect and get rid of their leaders as they saw fit. They had the right to freedom of speech, to freedom of religion, and to free assembly whenever they wanted to make their views heard. No government could take these rights from them, because they were spelled out in the Constitution that founded the United States.

Surprisingly, it all seemed to work. Across Europe, people began to see the United States as a model of how successful a revolution can be. They began to ask themselves—if it worked there, why not here?

THE PEOPLE OF FRANCE HAD SUFFERED FOR YEARS UNDER THE RULE OF A WEAK, UNCARING KING — THE SUCCESS OF THE AMERICAN REVOLUTION GAVE THEM THE INSPIRATION THEY NEEDED TO DO SOMETHING ABOUT IT.

THE FRENCH REVOLUTION BROUGHT MANY LONG-NEEDED REFORMS TO THE WAY THE COUNTRY WAS GOVERNED. BUT THE COST OF CHANGE WAS HIGH. IN THE UPHEAVAL THOUSANDS OF INNOCENT PEOPLE LOST THEIR LIVES.

POWER TO THE PEOPLE!

Illustrated by JUAN WIJNGAARD

FORTRESS FOUNDERS: Angry Parisians attack the Bastille in search of its store of gunpowder.

IN THE HOT DAYS of July 1789, the people of Paris finally lost patience with their King. On July 14, an enraged crowd attacked a royal fortress and started a revolution that shook the world. A reporter from *The History News* was there.

FOR MANY months now unrest has been brewing in France, and here in Paris anger has turned into action.

People tell me they are sick and tired of paying the huge taxes demanded by King Louis XVI and his advisors, while wealthy churchmen and nobles live idle, privileged lives and pay no taxes at all.

Everyone says that King Louis knows of his people's grievances but does nothing about them. Instead, rumor has it, he's moved his army into Paris in case of riots.

That rumor was the last straw. Two days ago a mob of frightened and angry Parisians raided the royal armory to steal hundreds of muskets.

Since then, the rebels have grown in number, and this morning a crowd of them gathered outside the Bastille — the royal fortress prison. The rebels wanted the Bastille's store of gunpowder to protect themselves from the King's troops. But the governor refused to hand it over.

As the day went on, more people joined the crowd, and tempers ran high. Then the rebels broke into the outer courtyard of the Bastille.

Guards stationed high on its ramparts began to fire down on the crowd, and a few people got shot.

That might have been the end of it, but to my amazement, a squad of soldiers turned up who seemed to side with the people. They had several cannons with them, which they aimed at the inner gates of the fortress. At this point the governor gave up and ordered his men to open the gates.

With a great roar the crowd stormed inside. Offices and storerooms were looted, and the few prisoners still held there were marched out of their cells as heroes.

TROUBLE LOOMS FOR LOUIS

All Paris is celebrating the storming of the Bastille — the city is drunk with joy at having challenged the King and won. And from the number of soldiers joining in, I'd say the King is in for a shock if he tries to use his army against the people in the future.

GREAT ESCAPE: The Bastille's prisoners are set free.

Bridgeman Art Library

UNJUST PRIVILEGES BITE THE DUST!

A FRENCH PARLIAMENT, the National Assembly, had formed in the spring of 1789. The King wasn't happy about it, but with so much unrest in the country he was forced to accept it. Then, to his horror, on August 4, 1789, the Assembly voted away many of the hated privileges of the nobility. The next day, *The History News* talked to one of its deputies — the nobleman, the Vicomte de Noailles.

❓ Nobody ever dreamed the nobles would give up their privileges. So what happened?

Well, we nobles can change with the times, too, you know. Last night, all of us in the Assembly — nobles, clergymen, and commoners — agreed to bury our differences.

We realized we had to make some sacrifices for the good of all the people of France. So we got rid of hundreds of old taxes and services that the peasants have had to give their landlords for centuries. Now everyone will pay their fair share of taxes, with no special exceptions.

❓ But why would you give up something that has made you rich?

You have to remember all the violence and rioting we've seen this summer. I believe that if we get rid of the unjust ways of the past — the ones the peasants object to most — we will have a better chance of restoring peace and order. We have to do something! We can't just behave like the King. He's carrying on as if nothing has happened — burying his head in the sand. We have to show the people that we mean business when we talk about "equal rights for all."

So what if I lose some of my income? It's worth it as long as people calm down and there is no more bloodshed.

❓ And if the rioters don't accept what the Assembly has done?

Good point — we nobles may have to give up still more of our privileges, I suppose.

The problem is, some of the revolutionaries are demanding that all of us, even the King, give up our titles and become citizens of France like everyone else. I don't think many nobles will want to do that, but if they don't, who knows where this terrible business will end? ❄

Jonty Clarke

The Clergyman   *The Nobleman*   *The Commoner*

ALL TOGETHER NOW: The new National Assembly speaks for all the people of France.

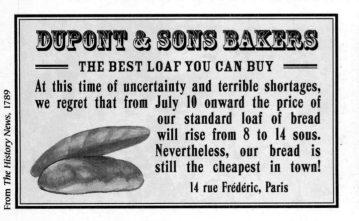

KING LOUIS TRIES TO FLEE FRANCE

UNNERVED BY the actions of the Assembly, King Louis shocked the country in 1791 when he secretly fled Paris to join his supporters abroad. *The History News* tracked down these witnesses and traced his flight.

Illustrated by CAROLINE CHURCH

Midnight, June 21, 1791

I was on guard duty the night the royal family ran away. A coach left the Palace at midnight and I saw someone inside it, dressed in a plain coat and wig. I thought he was just a visitor so I let him pass. But now I know it was a trick! It was the King in disguise.

A National Guardsman, Tuileries Palace

5:00 p.m., June 22, 1791

Today, I served some passengers in a huge green coach. As I passed in bowls of hot soup, I spied the King! But I said nothing. I never stick my nose into the affairs of travelers who stop here.

Innkeeper's wife, the Chalons posthouse

Also at 5:00 p.m., June 22, 1791

At midday, I rode with my troops to Pont de Somme-Vesle. We were to meet the King there and take him east to join his supporters. There was still no sign of the coach five hours later, so we left. We thought he had been unable to escape from Paris.

A Captain of the Royal Cavalry

8:00 p.m., June 22, 1791

I saw the King! It was just a glimpse as the coach went by, but I knew it was him. I checked his portrait on a 50-livre note and I was right. It was old fat face himself! So I rode like the wind to Varennes to raise the alarm, and at 11:00 P.M. we nabbed the lot of them!

Jean Drouet, Innkeeper, Saint-Ménehould posthouse

Morning, June 23, 1791

The travelers we halted late last night were indeed the King and his family. Two officials arrived this morning with an escort of the National Guard and armed citizens. They have taken the royal family back to Paris where their fate will be decided.

Maurice Sauce, Public Prosecutor, Varennes

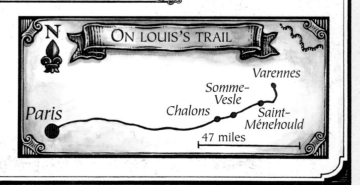

ON LOUIS'S TRAIL

Paris · Chalons · Somme-Vesle · Saint-Ménehould · Varennes

47 miles

KING OF FRANCE NO MORE

Illustrated by STEVE NOON

BETTER DAYS: Louis XVI before he lost his crown.

THE COUNTRY turned its back on Louis after his foolhardy attempt to run away. He was put on trial and found guilty of crimes against France. On January 17, 1793, he was sentenced to death. *The History News* spoke to him briefly in jail.

? **Sire, how have you been treated since you became a prisoner?**

Don't call me Sire! I'm not officially King anymore, and the guards get mad if anyone treats me as though I'm royalty.

My family and I were moved here to the Temple Fortress some months ago. As you can see, the rooms are bare and cold

— and the guards are loutish. They are always walking in and out — I have no privacy at all.

But I can bear all that. What is really monstrous is that I haven't been allowed to see my wife or my children since the start of my trial more than a month ago. That is definitely the worst part of this terrible ordeal.

? **Many people think of you as a tyrant and say the death sentence is a fitting end for you. Does this surprise you?**

Nothing surprises me any longer! But it's really not that simple. Ever since the National Assembly voted to make France a republic, it has wanted to make a clean break with anything royal.

The Assembly needs me out of the way so my supporters can't try to put me back on the throne.

? **What do you think will happen when you are gone?**

My main concern is for my family. They are no threat to anyone, yet I fear the worst. The new

authorities have already begun to send our closest friends and relatives to the guillotine.

As for the future of the nation, this passion for becoming a republic is fine for a young country such as America.

But history has shown time and time again that France needs one strong pair of hands at the helm. A republic has too many people trying to rule it — there'll be chaos, with Frenchman fighting Frenchman. Just look at what's happened already!

I fear the worst for France. The violence and bloodshed won't stop with my death. I'm quite sure of that.

DEATH OF A KING: Surrounded by soldiers, Louis is led to the guillotine. His body will be buried in an unmarked grave.

A TIME OF TERROR!

Illustrated by CHRIS MOLAN

ENEMIES EVERYWHERE: The government is arresting people for the slightest reason, even a chance remark. Nobody is safe.

LOUIS'S DEATH marked a change in the Revolution. France was under attack from its neighbors while its leaders fought each other for control of the country. Then things got worse, as these clippings from our news reports show.

SEPTEMBER 1793

The government's new Committee of Public Safety is now running the country. It has decreed a "reign of terror" against anyone who opposes its policies. This month alone it has accused so many people that all the jails are full. Special courts have been set up to try prisoners more quickly, and death sentences are being flung about like confetti. The leaders of the Committee include Maximilien Robespierre and Georges Danton — both powerful members of the government.

OCTOBER 1793

As of this month, any citizen has the authority to accuse another of treachery and have him or her arrested.

No one is safe. Even Marie Antoinette, widow of Louis XVI, has been beheaded along with 22 deputies of parliament who spoke out against the Terror.

NOVEMBER 1793

Philippe Capet, brother of Louis XVI, has been executed. In the city of Lyon, 64 prisoners, all said to be enemies of the Revolution, were shot.

DECEMBER 1793

All over France, nobles are being arrested and beheaded. The property of any noble who has fled abroad is instantly seized by the Committee.

JANUARY 1794

A peasant uprising in the Vendée, in western France, has been harshly crushed by supporters of the Revolution. Men, women, and children have been killed, and their villages burned as an example to protesters.

FEBRUARY 1794

News has just come in that all suspects arrested for crimes against the Revolution will have their property seized, whether they're found guilty or not.

MARCH 1794

The Committee itself is in turmoil! A group known as the Cordeliers was demanding even greater Terror measures against anyone who doubts the Revolution. Its members were promptly arrested and executed under the orders of Robespierre.

But when Committee member Georges Danton spoke out in favor of lessening the Terror, he and all of his supporters were arrested as well. And the orders for their arrest also came from Robespierre. It looks as if Robespierre is intent on taking complete control.

APRIL 1794

A few days ago, Danton and his supporters were tried and sentenced to death on the flimsiest of evidence. As he climbed the steps to the guillotine, Danton roared out that Robespierre would soon follow in his footsteps.

MAY 1794

The Terror reached a new height this month, when almost all of the early leaders of the Revolution were rounded up and sent to the guillotine.

JUNE 1794

There seems to be no end to the madness that is gripping France.

Robespierre and his supporters are arresting thousands of suspects — anyone, in fact, who might oppose him.

The number of arrests is so high that military barracks, hospitals, and even convents have been turned into jails. More people have been tried and executed in the last few weeks than in the past year.

JULY 1794

Robespierre himself has been arrested! Finally, sickened by the Terror, many committee members have lost their trust in him. His allies in the government have abandoned him and he will now face trial.

ROBESPIERRE: Young, gifted, and merciless.

TYRANT IS DEAD!

ON THE EVENING OF July 28, 1794, the brilliant but brutal Robespierre climbed the steps to the guillotine, and at last the Terror was brought to an end. *The History News* ran this report.

YESTERDAY, the most feared man in all of France was executed. Today, waves of relief swept through the country. Maximilien Robespierre is dead and now everyone hopes that the Terror will finally end.

It was fear that brought about his downfall. Anyone who'd stood in his way had been sentenced to death. Other members of government realized he would turn on them too, unless they moved first.

Just two days ago, officials accused him of acting like a tyrant and called for his arrest. Robespierre was immediately tried and then sentenced. Yesterday, he and 100 of his remaining followers were led to the guillotine.

When will the government also realize what a danger the Committee of Public Safety is and disband it?

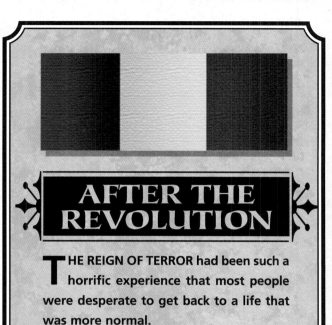

AFTER THE REVOLUTION

THE REIGN OF TERROR had been such a horrific experience that most people were desperate to get back to a life that was more normal.

AFTER ROBESPIERRE'S DEATH a new government was formed, but it was too weak to stop different groups from arguing about how the country should be run. In time, more and more people yearned for a strong leader who would put an end to the conflict and bring order back to France.

In 1799, a group of leaders turned to the army for support, and in particular to a successful young general called Napoleon Bonaparte. In November 1799, Bonaparte seized control of the government of France and brought the Revolution to an end.

But though the Revolution was over, it had changed France forever, and planted the seeds for what was to become the democratic country it is today.

It also had an enormous effect on the rest of Europe. People were no longer willing to accept the supreme right of a king to rule as he thought fit. In the future, no country's king or queen, or its nobles, would ever again feel completely safe.

THE FRENCH REVOLUTION led many people who were unhappy with their rulers to revolt too. Soon revolutions were happening all over the world — not all were a success, as these few examples demonstrate.

Illustrated by PETER VISSCHER

REVOLUTIONS

1804 HAITI: SLAVES GO FREE

In the rich, sugar-growing colony of Haiti, in the Caribbean, slaves outnumbered plantation owners by eight to one. In 1804, in a revolt against their harsh French masters, the slaves rose up and seized the towns and countryside. With their leader, Toussaint L'Ouverture, they overthrew the local government. France sent troops to crush the revolt and capture Toussaint. A few years later, though, Haiti became an independent country.

1819 COLOMBIA: LIBERATION

After years of Spanish rule, the colonies of South America longed for freedom like North America. After a string of battles their leader, Simón Bolívar, defeated the armies of Spain. He helped set up independent nations, first in Colombia, in 1819, and a few years later in Peru. He was so admired that Bolivia even took its name from him. Today his memory is still associated with liberty right across South America.

1848-1849
EUROPE: UP IN ARMS

In the space of a few weeks during the spring of 1848, revolution swept across Europe. In Paris and in the Austrian capital of Vienna, barricades were set up in the streets. In Germany, violent battles broke out in Berlin. In Hungary and Italy, movements to throw out foreign rulers began.

People were protesting the heavy-handed rule of kings and emperors. They called for elections and a say in how they were governed, either by setting up parliaments that worked hand in hand with monarchs, or by throwing out royal rulers and replacing them with a republic.

The old rulers fought back with energy and ruthlessness. Thousands of rebels lost their lives, and the uprisings fizzled out. But the old order was shaken, and some changes began to be made.

Haitian slaves take arms against colonists.

HAITI

COLOMBIA

Simón Bolívar, Colombia's freedom fighter.

N
W   E
S

1800–1905

Russia's Bloody Sunday starts peacefully.

Taiping rebels wage war on their rulers.

EUROPE

RUSSIA

Fighting breaks out in Vienna and across Europe.

INDIA

CHINA

Indian troops disobey British orders.

AUSTRALIA

Australian workers challenge British rule.

1851 CHINA: HEAVENLY REBELS

Manchu emperors ruled China for centuries, but in 1850 a schoolmaster led a rebellion that almost overthrew them. He set himself up in a village and called himself the Heavenly King of the Taiping. From there, his rebellion spread swiftly until it swallowed the city of Nanjing. It took 14 years and 20 million deaths before the imperial army crushed the rebels. The Taiping Rebellion had weakened the power of the Manchu emperors, but it couldn't topple them.

1851 AUSTRALIA: A MINER REVOLT

In the town of Ballarat in southern Australia, an angry protest over exorbitant fees for mining licenses turned into a rebellion against a heavy-handed government. It started with gold miners building a wooden fort — the Eureka Stockade — from which to fight the government of Australia, which was under British rule. Soon the miners were calling for a new parliament. Although the stockade fell to British troops, the miners did gain public support and forced their rulers to change some of their policies.

1857 INDIA: REBELLION

India was the jewel of the British Empire, though few Indians felt pleased about it. In 1857, there was a great rebellion of Indian troops who served in the British army. They rebelled against their orders and against the high-handed way the foreigners ruled India. The revolt lasted two years, and thousands died during it. After it was over, many Indians came to see it as the start of the struggle for independence that lasted almost 100 years.

1905 RUSSIA: NEAR REVOLUTION

In January, peaceful protesters in Russia were shot down by royal troops in what became known as the Bloody Sunday massacre. As news spread, the country went wild. There were strikes and protests everywhere, and in St. Petersburg workers set up a new city government. Finally, the Tsar, Nicholas II, sent his army to crush the rebels and nip the Revolution in the bud. Though he agreed to an elected parliament, the Duma, it had no real authority. The Tsar clung on to his power and stamped out the revolution.

HOT TIME IN A COLD TOWN!

IN FEBRUARY 1917, a huge crowd of women workers marched through St. Petersburg, then the capital of Russia, in protest against food shortages. Our reporter was there to witness the events that turned Russian history on its head.

AS IF THE hardships of World War I weren't bad enough, the winter here has been the coldest in years. Roads and railway lines have been blocked by ice and snow. The city is running out of fuel, bakers have no flour, and the people are hungry.

A few days ago, on February 23, the weather warmed a little to 23°F. As it was International Women's Day, a crowd of women cheerfully set off for the center of St. Petersburg to march for women's rights and to protest about the lack of bread and coal.

In the afternoon they were joined by many more women, coming from factories all over the city. In all, more than 100,000 people streamed into central St. Petersburg.

The city's police were unable to stop the march, so officials ordered a troop of tough Cossack soldiers to turn the women back. But the Cossacks refused to use force and let the high-spirited marchers pass in peace. That evening, the women returned home, amazed by the soldiers' decision and stunned by their own boldness.

The next day, an even larger crowd of both men and women flooded into the city. And the day after that, not one factory or workplace in the city stayed open as everyone joined the marchers.

TSAR GOES TOO FAR

There was a mood of determination in the air. People were openly waving banners reading "Down with the war" and even "Down with the

FEBRUARY MARCH: The people of St. Petersburg demonstrate their anger with the Tsar by parading through the center of the city.

OPEN FIRE: City police shoot into the crowds.

Illustrated by Mike White

NICHOLAS ABDICATES!

WHEN NICHOLAS II gave up the throne of Russia, 300 years of tradition vanished overnight. We recorded that turning point in Russian history with the following report from St. Petersburg.

Bridgeman Art Library

ON MARCH 2, 1917, a remarkable event took place in Russia. Just four days after losing control of his capital city, Tsar Nicholas II stepped down from the throne!

The news has been greeted with delight by the Russian people. And the Duma, the Russian parliament which had been largely ignored by the Tsar, has stepped in to fill the breach.

Clearly, the marching of the previous week finally blew the lid off a situation that has been brewing for years. Yet the Tsar responded to it with a typical act of carelessness. Ignoring the needs of his people, he chose to use force to crush their protests. This time, however, his decision backfired.

NO TROOPS, NO POWER

The army, which until now had always been loyal to the throne, was exhausted by war. Fighting an enemy was one thing, but killing their own people was without honor. When the soldiers refused to obey the Tsar's orders, the generals could do nothing about it.

Instead, they urged Nicholas to resign, and at last he realized he had no choice. His only option was to agree to give over the running of the country to a freely elected government, but he was so outraged by the idea he would not even consider it.

He thought he could hand the throne on, but his eldest son, Alexei, was far too frail to take over from his father. So in his abdication letter, Nicholas named his brother, Grand Duke Michael, as his heir.

Leaders of the Duma feared that their hopes for change were lost. But they did not have to worry for long. Grand Duke Michael had seen the riots in St. Petersburg and was not prepared to take the throne and risk his own life. Terrified, he fled the country.

At present, no one seems to know quite where the Tsar and his family have gone. But rumor has it that they may have been imprisoned for their own safety. ☭

RIA-Novosti/Sovfoto

WHERE ARE THEY NOW? Tsar Nicholas and his family.

Tsar." That's when Tsar Nicholas II made his big mistake.

He was at his country palace when he heard what was happening. But instead of returning to the city, he merely sent orders that his troops should use force to stop the protesters.

On the morning of Sunday, February 26, the city was swarming with armed soldiers as well as policemen. When the marchers neared the city center, the police opened fire on them. But instead of running, the crowd fought back bravely, and street battles broke out across the city.

TROOPS SIDE WITH THE PEOPLE

Over the next few hours, Tsar Nicholas lost control of the capital, as groups of soldiers refused to shoot at men and women who might well be their family or friends. Before long, all of the soldiers in St. Petersburg had disobeyed their orders and joined the marchers.

Together, soldiers and civilians took control of the city. They blocked off bridges and major crossroads to stop anyone entering or leaving.

Then, in a surge of fury against the hated city police, they attacked police stations and set them on fire.

By late Sunday night, the Revolution was in full flood. The people of St. Petersburg had risen up against their Tsar!

Nicholas ordered his generals to send other troops into the city. But knowing their men would side with the rebels, the generals refused. It looks as if there is nothing more the Tsar can do! ☭

HOME FOR THE PARTY: Lenin is greeted by his supporters in the Bolshevik Party as he arrives back in St. Petersburg.

David King Collection

LENIN RETURNS FOR REVOLUTION

ONCE THE TSAR had gone, a lot of exiled Russians came home. Among them was Vladimir Lenin, leader of the revolutionary group, the Bolshevik Party. Our reporter was at the station to meet him.

❓ How long have you been in exile, Mr. Lenin?
Far too long — since 1901. I was forced to flee Russia by the Tsar's police, who would have arrested me for being a revolutionary. I've missed my homeland a great deal, and it has been hard to be watched all the time by foreign police who thought I was

a troublemaker. But all of us in the Bolshevik Party never flagged in the task of working for a full-scale revolution here in Russia.

❓ But the Revolution started a month ago. Why has it taken you this long to come back?
It all happened sooner than we expected, or I'd

have come back weeks ago. But now, with this weak new government the Duma has set up and the war still dragging on, conditions are perfect for a true workers' revolution. Russia's workers, led by us of course, must seize power before it's too late.

❓ So what are your plans at this stage?
First, to meet with my comrades in the Bolshevik Party. We have to find a way of making it crystal clear to the people of Russia that we have to

pull out of the war now! Those imbeciles in the Provisional Government will ruin Russia with their plan to carry on fighting.

❓ And is that all the Bolsheviks want?
Of course not! We believe in the communist way — all land should be taken from the landowners and given to the peasants. And all industries should be run by the workers for the good of the workers. Basically our goals boil down to three things: "Peace, Land, and Bread!"

❓ What does the name "Bolshevik" mean, by the way?
It means "the majority" party — which is exactly what it will be once it has beaten its rivals. That's why I'm here, to make sure that it does! ☭

ON BEING BOLSHIE

With Lenin back, our political editor ran this handy guide to bring our readers up to date with who the Bolsheviks were:

1. The Bolsheviks are a revolutionary group. The Party was formed in England in 1903 after its founders, including Lenin, were chased out of Russia by the police — who realized they were working against the Tsar.

2. Bolsheviks take their ideas for a workers' revolution from the writings of the German thinker Karl Marx.

3. Their plan is to take control by an armed uprising. Then they will carry out their revolutionary ideals of taking wealth and power from the few in order to spread it among the many — the workers and the peasants of Russia.

4. The Bolsheviks want to abolish all private ownership of land, factories, and shops. Instead, all these things will be owned by the people.

PALACE TAKEN BY STORM

David King Collection

REBELS AT THE GATES: Lenin's Bolsheviks storm the Winter Palace, headquarters of the Provisional Government.

THE RUSSIAN Revolution took a surprising new turn in October 1917. *The History News* ran this account of the two days in which the Provisional Government was swiftly toppled from power.

EVERYONE in the city of St. Petersburg knew that the Bolshevik Party was planning something. Yet the government that had been in power since the fall of the Tsar refused to take the threat seriously.

On a freezing night on October 24, groups of armed Bolsheviks began to patrol the streets. They took control of the phone exchange, the main post office, railway stations, and the police stations.

Most people didn't even notice for a while — trains went on running, and the shops stayed open — but the Bolsheviks had taken command of the city.

UNLOVED AND UNWANTED

Although it had been popular at first, the Provisional Government had proved so ineffective, and its leader, Alexander Kerensky, so weak, that very few people saw any reasons for defending it.

The next day Kerensky realized the peril he and the rest of the government were in. In a last-minute attempt to find help, he left St. Petersburg to look for troops who might still be loyal.

But it was no use.

The Bolsheviks had made sure that St. Petersburg's soldiers and sailors were on their side before they struck. Kerensky didn't stand a chance! He never returned to the city.

The signal to attack the Winter Palace came a little after 9:30 P.M. The *Aurora*, a naval cruiser moored in the river nearby, fired a blank round. There was a deafening crash, and the Bolshevik troops rushed at the palace.

After that, however, there was more shouting than shooting. The palace guards had got fed up with hanging around all day without any orders and most had slipped away early for a meal. When the Bolsheviks swept in, there was no one to stop them.

Just after midnight, troops arrested the last few members of the Provisional Government, and Leon Trotsky, Lenin's co-leader, announced that the government had been replaced.

Seizing power wasn't hard for the Bolsheviks. The question now is, can they keep it? So far the other political groups are refusing to support them — they may yet have a fight on their hands. ☭

David King Collection

RUNNING THE SHOW

WHILE LENIN LED the Bolshevik Party to power, it was Leon Trotsky who made sure it stayed there. Trotsky was a brilliant organizer and he was willing to handle the toughest jobs. A year after the October Revolution, we asked him how things were going.

STIRRING STUFF: Posters spread the Bolshevik message to the far corners of Russia.

❓ What was the first task after the Party took power?

Well, once we controlled the two main cities, St. Petersburg and Moscow, our biggest problem was to end the war. As head of foreign affairs, it was my job to sign a peace treaty with the Germans. The Russian army was on the verge of collapse anyway, so we really had no choice.

❓ Why did you decide to change the country's capital to Moscow?

Two reasons, really. St. Petersburg is too close to the Russian border. When we were still at war with the Germans,

they managed to get uncomfortably near to the city during their last advance. Also, Lenin felt the capital should be farther east, closer to the heart of Russia.

❓ Is everyone glad to be out of the war?

Most people are, but there is still opposition

to the rest of our ideas, especially from the other political parties. We will not allow them to stand in our way, though, even if this means taking people's lives. You may think that's harsh, but what is an individual's life compared to the life of the Revolution? Earlier

this year, for example, it was necessary to have the Tsar and his family killed. We didn't want our enemies to try to put them back in power.

❓ But what about the workers themselves? Do they support you?

They do when they understand what we're

doing for them. It's vital that the workers know what this Revolution is about. That's why our Party members spend so much time helping to organize the masses by traveling around the country, giving lectures and showing films. And why we put so many posters up everywhere — the messages on them spread our ideas.

❓ Do you have any regrets so far?

None, though we still have a long struggle ahead of us. But, as Lenin always says, you have to have courage and absolute conviction to make a revolution.

Bridgeman Art Library

GONE BUT NOT FORGOTTEN: Lenin's image lives on.

AT REST IN RED SQUARE

WHEN LENIN DIED in January 1924, the Revolution still faced an uncertain future. In the midst of their mourning the question everyone asked was — who would take over from him?

RUSSIA is in shock today after hearing the news that its leader, Vladimir Ilyich Lenin, has died at the young age of 54.

Rumors about his failing health have been circulating for months, but no one, not even members of his own party, knew just how serious his illness was.

It's hard to imagine the Revolution without Lenin at its head. In spite of all the problems, he's kept it going for seven years now.

First he had to deal with the fact that the country had no money — the cost of fighting World War I had almost drained it dry.

Then came two years of fighting at home — against anti-communist groups. The Bolsheviks won, but Russia was in a mess. Lenin worked tirelessly to put the country back on its feet, but the strain of it ruined his health.

LOOKING FOR A LEADER

The Revolution still has a long way to go — and the Russian people are running out of patience — so it's not surprising that members of the Bolshevik Party are uneasy about its future. Who can possibly fill Lenin's shoes?

The History News has discovered that Lenin himself worried about this question. He feared that Party member Joseph Stalin would take his place, rather than someone like his old comrade, Leon Trotsky. Stalin is known to be ambitious and totally ruthless when it comes to getting his own way.

But such concerns are now a thing of the past for Lenin. Like a pharaoh of old, his body will be embalmed and placed in a great tomb in Moscow's Red Square, so that all Russians can come and pay their last respects to the "Father of the Revolution."

AFTER THE REVOLUTION

STALIN DID TAKE OVER after Lenin's death, and by 1929 he controlled what was then being called the Union of Soviet Socialist Republics (U.S.S.R.).

LENIN'S BOLSHEVIKS had fought their way to power in the name of Russian workers and peasants. It was the Bolsheviks' dream to give those who had nothing a fair share of the nation's wealth.

Under Stalin, though, whatever wealth the country had was owned and controlled by the government. People worked as hard as ever, but their lives had not improved. If anything, they were worse, as anyone who objected was either imprisoned or shot — and millions were.

For many Russians, then, the Revolution was a painful experience. But to many outsiders it seemed a wonderful new way to run a country. Communist parties flourished everywhere. In some places, they gained considerable support but never managed to take complete control. In others, such as China, they threw out old governments and replaced them with communist ones.

THE LONG MARCH TO FREEDOM

IN 1934, the Communist Red Army was a whisker away from being crushed by its rival, the Guomindang. To escape, it began a 6,000-mile march. Recently, we spoke to one of the last survivors of the Long March.

❓ Even today the Long March sounds like an incredible feat. Was it really necessary?

Absolutely! A well-armed Guomindang army was encircling and attacking us without a shred of mercy, so the choice was either move out or be wiped out. About 100,000 of us set off, marching in one fast-moving line. The line was a big mistake. It was so easy to attack us that within a mere ten weeks, our numbers had fallen to just 40,000.

❓ But why were you Communists and the Guomindang at each other's throats?

Civil wars are like that. Both sides wanted to lead China, but in totally different ways. Most people in China are peasant farmers, and we believed that they held the answer to China's problems. If we could unite them and get them to fight for us, we could sweep away our enemies. Once we'd done that we could take the land from

KEEPING IN STEP: Communists follow their new leader Mao Zedong across China.

William MacQuitty

the rich landowners and give it to the peasants who worked on it.

But the Guomindang hated our ideas. They needed the big landlords and the rich people in the cities to support them. So they wanted to destroy us before we got too strong.

❓ What was it like on the Long March?

In a word — terrible! After we left southern China, we spent a whole year zigzagging across the country, trying to avoid the enemy. Many of us died from illness, hunger, or just sheer exhaustion.

By the time we arrived in the northwest province of Shaanxi, there were only 8,000 of us left. The worst moment I recall was trying to cross the Luding Bridge. Every time we set foot on the bridge, enemy guns mowed us down. In the end, some volunteers crawled along chains underneath the bridge and captured the road on the other side.

❓ What about your leaders? Did they do a good job?

Well, at first we had several leaders, but then Mao Zedong took over.

He knew exactly where to go, although by marching us day after day to escape from enemy troops he all but killed us.

❓ Yet the March was a success in the end.

Yes, although we only made it to Shaanxi by the skin of our teeth. But at least we could stop there and build the revolution we wanted — among the peasants. Luckily for us, the Guomindang became so busy fighting Japan they left us alone. And that gave us time to get organized and build up our army again. ★

Eastfoto

TOUGH GOING: The Red Army struggles to safety.

WHAT'S IT ALL ABOUT?

WHEN NEWS of the Long March came out, we had a lot of letters asking us what was going on. Here is a typical letter and our response to it.

Dear Sir,
Little news of what's really going on in China ever leaks out. We know the country is in the middle of a power struggle, but we don't have a clue who's involved. Can you tell us a bit more about it?
H. Jones, Chicago, Ill.

Dear Mr. Jones,
There are basically two opposing forces. On one side is the Communist Party, led by Mao Zedong.

Mao's beliefs are much the same as those of the Russian Communists except that, unlike them, his revolution is based in the countryside. In his opinion, peasants are more willing to fight than city people, and can endure more

hardship — perhaps because they have less to lose.

The other side, the Guomindang, is led by Chiang Kai Shek. His party officially governs China now, and it relies on the support of wealthy landlords and rich city people. At the moment, the Japanese army is giving him big problems.

Back in 1931, China was invaded by the Japanese. In the last few years, they have taken over a large part of the northeast. The Japanese are hated so much that the Communists and the Guomindang have called a truce in order to fight them, but when it's all over, the two sides will still be enemies. ★

Sovfoto/Eastfoto

TUG OF WAR: Mao (left) and Chiang Kai Shek both want the same thing — China.

THE GREAT DEBATE

BACK IN 1937, *The History News* invited Mao Zedong and Chiang Kai Shek to tell our readers about their plans for China — they could not have been more different.

MAO ZEDONG

Do you know why China is so poor and weak? It's because the officials in the cities are corrupt and feeble. They don't know which way to turn, and they're afraid to make the tough decisions our country needs to get ahead. Instead, they rely too much on foreign help.

China's strength is in the hundreds of millions of peasants who live on the land. The Communist Party knows that, and we know what's best for them, too, because we listen to what they say. We know how to use

their strength to rebuild the nation. That's why the first thing we'll do when we come into power is seize all land from the privileged few and divide it up fairly among the peasants. Everyone will have some land.

CHIANG KAI SHEK

The Guomindang is the best party to lead China. It is strong in the cities where the wealth and knowledge lie to turn

China into a rich and powerful country.

If you think clueless country bumpkins hold the secret to the future, you should think again. Leadership comes from those of us who look out to the rest of the world.

We understand how to go about building a thriving nation, just like our friends in America. What's more, they will lend us the money to set up new factories to create jobs and wealth. There's only one thing in our way — the Japanese invaders. Once we've driven them out of China we can put a stop to this Communist Party nonsense, too. Then the way to a prosperous future will be clear. ★

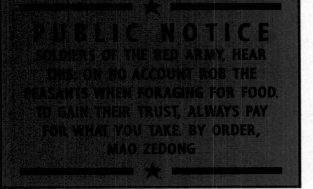

From *The History News*, 1970

PUBLIC NOTICE
SOLDIERS OF THE RED ARMY, HEAR THIS. ON NO ACCOUNT ROB THE PEASANTS WHEN FORAGING FOR FOOD. TO GAIN THEIR TRUST, ALWAYS PAY FOR WHAT YOU TAKE. BY ORDER, MAO ZEDONG

MAO MARCHES IN TO CAPTURE

SHOW OF STRENGTH: Mao salutes his victorious troops in Beijing's Tiananmen Square.

ON A WINDSWEPT February day in 1949, the Red Army marched into Beijing, the capital of China. After years of bitter fighting, it had finally won. At the time, our reporter recalled how a scruffy, half-starved army had become the military machine that unified China.

AS I WATCHED the Red Army streaming past, I couldn't help but think back to 1936. In those days a Red Army parade would have been over in minutes, not hours!

Yet just four years later, the Communists' troops were half a million strong and a force to be reckoned with. Today, the Red Army is triumphant — promising a bright future under its leader, Chairman Mao.

When the war with Japan was at its height, from 1937 to 1945, it took every last ounce of both the Communists' and the Guomindang's resources. Yet it also allowed the Communist Party a once in a lifetime chance to grow. Party members and soldiers traveled across northern China in small groups, spreading Mao's message. They even went into Japanese-held areas to live and work with the peasants there.

By their actions the Red Army soldiers showed people how Communism could mean hope for a better future. Peasants soon began to join the Red Army in droves, especially in areas under Japanese control. It was their chance to hit back at the invaders who made their lives a misery.

The war was tougher on the Guomindang. It lost many of its best troops and equipment to the Japanese. Its leaders squabbled among themselves, and its officials became lazy and weak.

A CHANGE OF FORTUNE

When Japan was finally defeated, the two old enemies turned on each other once more. Civil war broke out again, only this time it went badly for the Guomindang. Its soldiers simply didn't have the discipline and fierce commitment of the Communist troops.

By 1948, the Red Army had gained the upper hand almost everywhere. And now, just one year later, the Guomindang has fallen, and the surviving shreds of its army are fleeing to the nearby island of Taiwan.

So what lies ahead for the Red Army and for China? At the moment, everyone is full of praise for Mao. Ordinary people all over the country are eagerly awaiting the time when he will put his long-promised plans into action. Then land will be taken from the rich and given to the peasants who spend their days actually working on it.

THE CAPITAL

Mary Evans Picture Library

Everyone is excited, too, about Mao's plans to reorganize the factories, and to make them bigger and more efficient. For a nation of people still suffering from the after-effects of war and famine, it sounds almost too good to be true.

Today, as the troops known as the "People's Liberation Army" proudly laid claim to the city of Beijing, those of us who watched them cannot doubt that a new era is about to dawn.

All that remains is to see if the Communist Party can change China's fortunes and turn it into a country where every-one has enough to eat. In other words, can Mao keep his promises? ★

ONE STEP FORWARD, TWO STEPS BACK!

THE COMMUNISTS were just getting China back on its feet when, in 1958, Mao decided the country could do better. He called his idea the Great Leap Forward. Some years later a retired factory worker gave us her view of it.

WE WERE thrilled about the Great Leap at first. Mao said we could build China much faster if we rolled up our sleeves and gave it everything we had. We would be rich in only 15 years, he said. It sounded so good no one realized how risky it was.

Early in 1958, tens of millions of peasants set to work digging irrigation ditches to carry more water to the crops. The peasants dug day and night — but they began to neglect all their other farming chores.

The rest of us were expected to build small furnaces at home or at work to make iron. If we had no iron ore, we melted down old pots and tools. No matter who we were — doctor, factory worker, teacher — we all spent hours making iron. But few of us knew what we were doing, so the metal we produced was impure. Most of it was useless.

Everyone was doing so much extra work that

LEAP OF FAITH: Office workers struggle to make iron.

Eastfoto

they were ignoring their main jobs. As a result, the next harvest was a disaster, and officials lied to cover up how badly the new plan was going.

By 1960, China had run out of food. About twenty million people starved to death that year, and we had to buy our grain from abroad.

Mao's great idea was so poorly planned that our farms collapsed and factories produced half the amount they had before. In fact, the Great Leap took us backward, not forward. ★

PUBLIC NOTICE

COMRADES!
A REVOLUTION IS BUILT
WITH IRON AND STEEL,
SO TAKE TIME TODAY TO
TEND TO YOUR FURNACE.
BY ORDER OF
CHAIRMAN MAO.

From *The History News*, 1962

CULTURE SHOCK!

AFTER THE FAILURE of the Great Leap, Mao wanted to show China he was still in charge. His answer was the Cultural Revolution, a reign of terror that shook China to the core. Only now is it safe to print these stories of what it was like.

★ STUDENT

I was 16 in 1966, when the Cultural Revolution began. My friends and I weren't even born when Mao first took power. But we still felt like true revolutionaries when we answered his call to attack those in authority who had forgotten what the Revolution was about.

First, we turned on our teachers for caring more about education than the Revolution. We shouted at them and beat them. We chased them out of the classrooms. Then we did the same to the Party officials. They thought they were above criticism, so we threw them all out!

★ PARTY OFFICIAL

I had been a Party official since 1940, and I was shocked when students began attacking Party members during the Cultural Revolution. The students called them- selves Red Guards and behaved in a terrible way. They humiliated us and wrecked the work we were doing. Other officials and even our families were too scared to show support for us. We were forced to leave our homes and work with the peasants. It was appalling.

Mary Evans Picture Library

HARD LABOR: City people learn to work on the land.

If the army hadn't begun to restore order, who knows what would have happened to China?

★ TEACHER

I taught literature in college for many years. Now I can only find work as a night watchman. The schools and universities were all closed after the Red Guards invaded them at the start of the Cultural Revolution. The Guards spat at us and beat us. Many people were beaten so badly they died. My students mocked me in public for owning books. They called me filthy names. Even my own children turned against me. I tried to understand why my ideas were so wrong, but I couldn't.

Many of us lost hope. Our spirits were broken. When the universities started to open again, I couldn't face going back. The Cultural Revolution was a madness that had almost ruined China. ★

Popperfoto

HUMILIATED: Party officials are paraded in public as enemies of the Revolution.

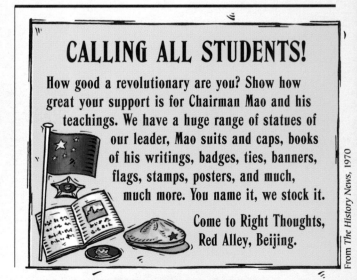

David King Collection

OUR HERO: The youth of China clasp Mao's Little Red Book to their hearts.

DEATH OF THE CHAIRMAN

MAO WAS IN poor health for many years, yet he ruled China with an iron hand until his last breath. When he died in 1976, at age 83, *The History News* looked back at the life of the man who was the father of the Chinese Revolution.

NO MATTER how you think of Mao Zedong — as a tyrant or a genius — it is clear that the effect he has had on China has been vast.

His followers called him "Great Leader" and "Great Inspiration." Mao called himself simply "a man of the people," yet he never denied the praise that was heaped on him. For the son of a peasant to become the leader of a billion people is a spectacular rise up the ladder of life.

The climb to the top, and staying there,

wasn't easy. Mao first had to convince his Communist colleagues that a revolution fought by armies of peasants could be as successful as that fought by the factory workers in Russia. Then he had to teach the rest of China that a revolution isn't made overnight, but takes long years of hard work to complete.

REBUILDING CHINA

Before the Revolution, China was weak and divided. Various leaders grabbed whatever they could and squabbled over the rest, with no thought for the well-being

of their people. Under Mao, China became one nation again, with a strong army and a more efficient, hardworking government.

Mao was a harsh and demanding leader, and often changed his mind as if on a whim. He treated millions of Chinese as enemies and with appalling cruelty. But for millions more he was a hero who could do no wrong. While he lived, the teachings in his *Little Red Book* were learned by heart and became the rules that people lived by.

Mao's shadow still looms over China. But for how much longer remains to be seen. ★

AFTER THE REVOLUTION

AS MAO WAS REACHING THE END of his rule, the rest of the world finally began to recognize that the People's Republic of China was here to stay. Canada, the United States, and several other western nations sent ambassadors to China, and in 1971 the People's Republic became a member of the United Nations.

AFTER MAO'S DEATH, a struggle for power broke out in the Communist Party. On one side were the Radicals — who totally supported all of Mao's ideas and wanted China to stick strictly to his plans. On the other were the Moderates — who honored Mao but believed that China needed more practical ways of governing such huge numbers of people, and more contact with the outside world. The Moderates won and have led the country ever since.

Mao's great vision was his belief that the millions of uneducated and largely ignored peasants in China could help to change their country and their own lives. The Chinese Revolution was so sweeping that peasants in countries all over the world began to think that they, too, could start a revolution!

DOWN WITH THE WALL

LARGE-SCALE, violent, full-blown revolutions have been with us for more than 300 years. The question is: Will there be more in the future? We asked a professor of history who has studied revolutions for years to give us an idea of what to expect.

Will there be more violent revolutions like those in Russia or in China?

Perhaps, but the heyday of big, violent upheavals like those two is probably over. And for two good reasons.

The first is that both these revolutions were inspired by communist ideas that workers and peasants would rise up and take control of government. Well, now we've had communist governments for much of the twentieth century. The experiment created more problems than it solved. People came to see that a communist system was no way to run a prosperous country.

The second reason they are over is that the world is much more close-knit than it was 100 years ago. Nations trade with one another and depend on one another more than ever before. So it's harder for a country to go it alone without other nations getting dragged into the struggle too.

UNITED AGAIN: In 1989, ordinary Berliners finally knock down the hated Wall.

CUT IN TWO: The Berlin Wall divided the city in 1961.

Back in 1989 there were upheavals in Eastern Europe as countries turned their backs on Communism. Do these count as revolutions?

Oh, yes. But they're a new kind. Instead of killing millions, they merely scrapped the old system of government.

There were plenty of protests as peaceful crowds took to the streets, yet hardly any bloodshed. The old communist order had lost its will to continue because so few citizens in East Germany, Poland, or Czechoslovakia believed in it anymore. Nowhere was this more powerfully symbolized than in the knocking down of the Berlin Wall, which had divided communist from democratic Germany.

Within weeks, many ex-leaders were thrown in jail while the people they once locked up now ran the government. We all learned from this that there can be revolutions without bloodshed.

Does that mean future revolutions will be more peaceful, too?

We probably won't see any more communist revolutions. But if a government is unable, or unwilling, to cope with the needs of its people there is always a chance that a revolution will boil up from below.

Whether more peaceful or more violent is hard to say. I would guess more peaceful. One thing will always be true — the trouble with revolutions is that they are so unpredictable. ◪

1765
In London, Parliament passes the Stamp Act to tax American colonies.

1773
At the Boston Tea Party (a protest against British tax levels) shiploads of tea are dumped into Boston Harbor.

1775
Revolution begins when British troops clash with American minutemen at Lexington.

1776
Delegates of the Continental Congress adopt the Declaration of Independence.

1778
France agrees to help the American colonies in their fight against Britain.

1781
A British army surrenders at Yorktown, and the fighting comes to an end.

1783
By the Treaty of Paris, Britain finally recognizes America's independence.

1788
Louis XVI of France calls a meeting of the national parliament for May, 1789, to deal with the nation's crippling debts.

1789
In France, crowds storm the Bastille, triggering the start of the French Revolution.

In the United States, George Washington is named first president. ▼

1791
Louis XVI flees the Revolution. He is caught and brought back.

1792
With the King in prison, awaiting execution, France becomes a republic.

1793
King Louis XVI of France is executed, and the Reign of Terror starts. Marie Antoinette and the King's family are also executed. ▼

1794
Maximilien Robespierre is executed, and the Terror starts to wind down.

1804
A slave uprising in Haiti leads to its independence from France.

1819
In South America, after a revolution against Spain, Símon Bolívar becomes first president of Colombia.

1848
Revolutions break out in Vienna and Frankfurt. Both are crushed.

1849
Hungary declares itself to be independent from Austria. The Revolution is stamped out by Austrian and Russian armies.

1851
The Taiping Rebellion in China fails to establish a new government.

1854
A revolt among miners in Australia, known as the Eureka Stockade, opposes the government of the colony, but it is crushed by British troops.

1905
A workers' uprising in St. Petersburg is crushed in a clash known as Bloody Sunday. The country lurches toward revolution until the army crushes it.

1917
The February Revolution takes place in Russia. The Tsar steps down. Eight months later, in the October Revolution, Lenin becomes head of a communist government.

1918
Russia signs a treaty with Germany and withdraws from World War I.

1919
The Red Army, led by Lenin, becomes the most powerful group in Russia.

1920
The Russian Civil War ends with victory for Lenin. The Communist Party now controls Russia.

1924
In Russia, Lenin dies. His body is embalmed and placed in a museum. ▼

1934
The Long March begins as Chinese Communists escape from Chiang Kai Shek's nationalist army.

1937
Both Communists and Nationalists in China fight the Japanese armies that are invading.

1945
Japan is defeated at the end of World War II. The Nationalists and Communists in China start to fight again.

1949
Chiang Kai Shek resigns as president of China. The communist People's Republic of China is declared with Mao Zedong as its leader. ▼

1961
The Berlin Wall goes up to separate West Berlin from the communist East and prevent people on each side from mixing.

1966
The Cultural Revolution begins in China and lasts four years.

1976
In China, Chairman Mao Zedong dies.

1989
The Berlin Wall falls. Peaceful revolutions sweep eastern Europe and defeat communism.

★★★★★★ INDEX ★★★★★★

A
America 3–9, 13
Antoinette, Marie 14, 31
Army, Red 24, 25, 26
Army, People's Liberation 26, 27
Australia 17, 31
Austria 16, 31

B
Bastille 10, 31
Berlin Wall 30, 31
bloodshed 11, 13
Bloody Sunday 17, 31
Bolívar, Simón 16, 31
Bolsheviks 20, 21, 22, 23
Boston Tea Party 3, 4, 31
British 3, 4, 5, 6, 7, 8, 17, 31

C
Capet, Philippe 14
Chiang Kai Shek 25, 31
China 17, 24–29, 30, 31
Chinese Civil War 26
clergy 10, 11
Colombia 16, 31
Committee of Public Safety 14
Common Sense 4
Communism 20, 23, 24, 25, 26, 27, 29, 30, 31
Congress 9
Cordeliers 14
Cornwallis, General 7
Cossacks 18
Cultural Revolution 28, 31

D, E
Danton, Georges 14–15
Dawes, Will 4
Declaration of Independence 5, 31
de Grasse, Admiral 7
Eureka Stockade 17, 31

F, G
France 6, 7, 8, 10–15, 16, 31

George III, King 3, 4, 5, 8
Germany 16, 31
Great Leap Forward 27, 28, 31
guillotine 13, 15
gunpowder 10
Guomindang 24, 25, 26

H, I, J
Haiti 16, 31
Hungary 16, 31
India 17
Japan 24, 25, 26
Jefferson, Thomas 5

K, L
Kerensky, Alexander 21
Lenin, V. I. 20, 21, 22, 23, 31
Long March, The 24, 25, 31
Louis XVI, King 10, 11, 12, 13, 14, 31
loyalist 5, 8

M
Manchu emperors 17
Mao Zedong 24, 25, 26, 27, 28, 29, 31
Marx, Karl 20
Minutemen 4
Mohawk Indians 3

N, O
National Assembly 11, 13
Nicholas II, Tsar 17, 18, 19, 20, 21, 22, 31
Noailles, Vicomte de 11
nobles 10, 11, 14, 15
October Revolution 21, 31

P, Q
Paine, Tom 4
patriot 4, 5, 8
peasants 11, 20, 24, 25, 27, 29
Prescott, Doctor Sam 4

President George Washington 9, 31
Provisional Government 20, 21

R
rebels 10
redcoats 4, 7
republics 9, 13, 29, 31
Revere, Paul 4
Robespierre, Maximilien 14, 15, 31
Russia 17, 18–23, 24, 29, 30, 31

S
Stalin, Joseph 23
St. Petersburg 17, 18, 19, 20, 21, 22, 31

T
Taiping Rebellion 17, 31
taxes 3, 4, 5, 10, 11
Terror, the 14–15, 31
Toussaint L'Ouverture 16
Treaty of Paris 8, 31
troops 3, 4, 7, 8, 19, 26–27
Trotsky, Leon 20, 21, 22, 23, 31
Tsar 17, 18, 19, 20, 21, 22, 31

U, V
Valley Forge 6
Varennes 12

W
Washington, George 6, 7, 8, 9, 31
Winter Palace 21
Women's Day, International 18
World War I 18, 23, 31

X, Y, Z
Yorktown, Battle at 7, 8, 31

Author: Christopher Maynard
Consultant: Dr. Tim Shakesby, King's College Cambridge
Editor: Anderley Moore
Designer: Jonathan Hair

Ads and small illustrations by: Bridgeman Art Library: Pennsylvania Academy of Fine Arts USA 9tl; Musée Carnavalet, Paris/Giraudon 10bl; Prado, Madrid 13tr; Christie's Images, London 19tr; Caroline Church: 1; David King Collection: 31br Roy Miles Esq. 23tl; Ian Thompson: 26bl, 28br; Mike White: 4tr, 8, 11.

With thanks to: Artist Partners, Beehive Illustration, Illustration Limited, Temple Rogers

Text copyright © 1999 by Christopher Maynard Illustrations copyright © 1999 by Walker Books Ltd.

All rights reserved.

First U.S. edition 1999

Library of Congress Cataloging-in-Publication Data is available.

ISBN 0-7636-0491-7

2 4 6 8 10 9 7 5 3 1

Printed in Hong Kong

This book was typeset in Tiepolo.

Candlewick Press 2067 Massachusetts Avenue, Cambridge, Massachusetts 02140

SOURCES

John R. Alden, *The American Revolution*
Mark Almond, *Revolution — 500 Years of Struggle for Change*
Lucien Bianco, *The Chinese Revolutions*
Edward Countryman, *The American Revolution*
William Doyle, *The Oxford History of the French Revolution*
John Dunn, *Modern Revolutions*
Marc Ferro, *October 1917*
Orlando Figes, *A People's Tragedy: The Russian Revolution, 1891–1924*
Sheila Fitzpatrick, *The Russian Revolution*
Jack Gray, *Rebellions and Revolutions, China from the 1800s to the 1980s*
Michael S. Kimmel, *Revolution, A Sociological Interpretation*
Maurice Meisner, *Mao's China and After*
Simon Schama, *Citizens*
Robert Service, *The Russian Revolution*
Jonathan Spence, *The Search for Modern China*
D.M.H. Sutherland, *France 1789–1815*
Morton White, *The Philosophy of the American Revolution*